SECOND WIND

SECOND WIND

PATRICIA FROLANDER

HIGH PLAINS PRESS

Poetry of the American West Series

Cover photograph © Shutterstock, Ross Taylor artist

FIRST PRINTING

1 3 5 7 9 8 6 4 2

The Wyoming bucking horse and rider trademark
is federally registered by the State of Wyoming
and is licensed for restricted use through the Secretary of State's office.

Library of Congress Cataloging-in-Publication Data

Names: Frolander, Patricia, author.
Title: Second wind / Patricia Frolander.
Description: Glendo, WY : High Plains Press, [2020] | Series: Poetry of the
    American West | Summary: "A collection of poems by Patricia Frolander.
    She writes of loss, aging, and life on a ranch in the Black Hills of
    northeast Wyoming." -- Provided by publisher.
Identifiers: LCCN 2020004696 | ISBN 9781937147051 (trade paperback)
Subjects: LCGFT: Poetry.
Classification: LCC PS3606.R5845 S43 2020 | DDC 811/.6--dc23
LC record available at https://lccn.loc.gov/2020004696

HIGH PLAINS PRESS
403 Cassa Road
Glendo, WY 82213
1-800-552-7819

Catalog available.
www.highplainspress.com

To my irreplaceable family
and the incredible Bearlodge Writers.

CONTENTS

Preface: Transitions   ix

OLD PASTURE

Dowry   12
Bernice   14
Missouri Buttes   15
Banquets   16
Embers   17
Pedigree   18
The Game   19
Bequest   20
Harvest   21
Branch of the Family Tree   22
Thistles   23
Saddlemaker   24
The Silver Belly   25
Accidents Happen   26
Enchantment   28
Hot Dogs by Candlelight   29
Salvage   30
Kinfolk   31
Heartwood   32

DROUGHT

Prairie Reclamation   34
For Sale   35
Empty Harness   36
Discarded   37
Fried Bread   38
Transfer   39
Hollow   40
Euthanasia   41
The Millionaire   42
Baptism   43

Coroner's Report   44
Widow's Wait   45
Bittersweet   46
Atlas   47
End of the Season   48
Congestive Heart   49
Years Slipped Away   50
Widowmaker   51
Departure   52
Lilacs   53
Dream Watch   54

FRESH GRASS

Yesterday's Soldiers   56
Red-headed Trouble   58
Dusk   59
Big Horn Mountains   60
Away   61
The Last Mile   62
Weakness of the Mind   63
A Mother's Will   64
Awakening   65
Riding the Edge of Goodbye   66
Tending Wild Horses   67
Delivering Flowers to the Nursing Home   68
Solstice   69
Benediction   70
Talisman   71
Retreat   72
Seasoned   73
Cowboy Cafe   74
Winter Garden   75
Prayer Stars   76
Who Would I Be if I Didn't Have a Name?   77

PREFACE: TRANSITIONS

After fifty-three years of marriage, my husband's heart disease claimed him. We worked this fifth generation ranch together for forty-seven years, and I miss him more than words can express.

Our grown children and grandchildren have their own lives. Although I see them often, the shift is apparent. They warn me about ladders, horses, viruses, and icy roads. I smile in gratitude for their concern and perhaps grit my teeth occasionally.

Ranch pastures still govern my life. Old pastures, with last year's growth of grass, can be a lifesaver in drought. Of course, ranchers want mature, well-cured grass and alfalfa hay for their winter forage supply. A new stand of green succulent grass—well, that's the hope for the future.

Although calving, fencing, and haying no longer physically define my days, I continue to manage the ranch. I have more time to write, read, explore this upthrust of the Black Hills. Most importantly, I make more time for family, friends, and prayer.

Stop by, have coffee, and we'll go look for some fresh grass.

Old Pasture

DOWRY

Great-Granddad Belshe wedged
a one-room cookshack onto logs
and tied it down. His horses leaned
into their harness, slogged seven miles
to his ranch where he placed it on
a stone foundation.

His daughter
patched, painted, and prettied
as winter winds whistled
through the added porch and lean-to.
The cherry red potbelly stove struggled
to melt ice etched on glassed windows.

Among her suitors, one gifted his heart.
Hollyhocks adorned her veil
as she married in the front yard.
Days passed into years.
Children, grandchildren, greats,
passed the deed from generation to generation.

Over a hundred years of springtime
since roof was placed, stovepipe set.
The sandstone foundation splits and crumbles;
floor tilts, and bedsprings rust.
A wringer washer slumps on the porch.
Chickens roost in the lean-to.
The stove stands cold, layered in soot.
Birds fly in and out of broken windowpanes.

This year we lay the old girl to rest.
Heavy snows signal the match.
A dowry lost in smoke and ash—
hollyhocks may survive.

BERNICE

My neighbor draws this city-bred, young ranch wife,
into her sun-drenched kitchen.
Between snippets of Scripture and shared recipes,
I learn the history of Houston Creek, Wyoming.

She pulls her rolling pin from a stubborn drawer,
speaks of threshing bees, Mormon crickets,
and fires raging through droughty fields.
Apron-draped, she throws a handful of flour,
then another, texture guiding her hands.

Tales of illness and accidents blend with
cornstarch, water, eggs, lemon, and sugar.
Meringue turns golden as stories of weddings,
neighbors' quarrels, and all-night dances
carry me to another place in time.

Oatmeal cookies, with plumped raisins,
meet a hint of nutmeg in her chipped bowl.
She tells me of her first beau, the man she wed,
the loss of their child. She hums hymns,
spoons the dough onto the cookie sheet.

On Thanksgiving, she gives me a pie
from garden pumpkin steamed soft,
blended with cinnamon, cloves,
ginger, butter, sugar, and flour.
I plant pumpkin the following spring.

Jotted recipes fade, but I know them by heart
like her stories,
the Twenty-Third Psalm,
and the sweetest taste of fellowship.

MISSOURI BUTTES

Sunlight lazes on hillsides burdened with pine.
Shadowed draws veil bedded bucks.
Missouri Buttes cast watchful eyes,
approve the spring surge of the Belle Fourche,
behold their sibling Mato Tipila, Devils Tower.

Natives and pioneers claim this sacred place,
their powers ephemeral
as are mine against
layers of snow, summer rains, insistent winds.
Soon more bones will inlay in sandstone,
partner with belemnites for eternity.
The Buttes bear witness.

BANQUETS

Belgians warm their heavy frames
forging a trail through
snow-covered feed grounds.
Cows rise from their beds
on yesterday's leftover fodder.

The hay-laden sleigh catches
on frozen piles of manure,
lurches ahead, as expectant ruminants
maneuver their swollen bellies
around one another.

As I pitch alfalfa onto fresh snow,
bovine breath vapors in morning air.
Ice crackles and snaps beneath
slick runners of the sled.
Clouds obscure the sun.

Five saddle horses, snow flying
beneath trim bellies, skid to a stop
at the upper gate, wait impatiently
for their morning banquet. Soft nickers
float on the morning breeze.

Feeding finished, team and sled
arc the pasture toward home.
I lean into my husband as he deftly
handles the reins, winter days
running before us.

EMBERS

Outside our bedroom window,
Hunter's Moon ascends,
shadows a palace of ice.
I lie beside you, snug,
warmed by your body.
Aged hands clasp.

Another moonlit night,
summers ago,
hip and shoulder, smooth skin,
curved against a crumpled sheet.
Younger bodies twined,
breath heavy, moist warmth filled the air.

Passion's ebb and flow diminish
with decades, but never doubt
a banked fire burns—
an unexpected smile, touch,
quickens the blood, excites the heart,
ignites the heat.

PEDIGREE

Ponderosas surround quaking aspen. Dark needles
counterpoint smooth pale bark scarred in black.
Carved initials blemish horizontal bands and knots.
Butter-gold leaves tremble, their flattened petioles

lift in the western breeze.
Roots plunge deep into the earth,
hidden cambium carries xylem and phloem,
increase your girth ever so slowly.

Natives boiled your inner bark, cured illness.
Now books, fine paper, furniture bear
your signature, as do autumn mountains
punctuated in golden splendor.

Centuries will pass—
pine will litter the forest floor
while your roots bundle,
ancestor to ancestor.

THE GAME

She's six, I'm sixty;
and know she's the best
I've ever saddled.

She's trying to avoid me
by hiding in the brush,
moving away as I push forward.

So easy to follow her buckskin body
slipping with grace through the draw,
surging up the other side.

Nostrils flaring, tail held high,
she's fanning me goodbye.
I mutter epithets.

I scan the trees, inhale their fragrance,
hear her nicker, and smile,
despite sharp air invading my coat.

Game over,
she lopes to the barn,
perhaps wondering if I'll give her grain.

BEQUEST

In Memory of Bertha Frolander

During the Depression,
Grandma cooked for loggers three times a day;
grateful to feed her son and daughter,
grateful for a place to lay her head.
She hauled wood until her arms could hold no more,
stoked the fire, stood pigeon-toed
before the Home Comfort as she fried bacon and eggs.
Come noon, fried chicken and gravy filled hungry bellies.

Humid afternoons she canned beans, tomatoes, or pickles,
beads of perspiration on her lip. That stove never cooled.
Grandma's spoon, worn down on one side,
stirred applesauce to 'just right,' her little girl watching.
The baby cooed as Gran shucked corn and boiled beans.

Worn dollar bills were tucked each month into an old sock.
Her spoon kept stirring and her children kept sprouting.
Clothes mended, new shoes for growing feet,
Grandma's thin leather must last another year.
She stuffed bits of paper inside the soles for warmth.

Today the Home Comfort is stored in my shed.
Grandma and her children rest in a hillside cemetery.
On my electric stove, I stir the applesauce
to 'just right' with the spoon worn down on one side,
stand pigeon-toed as I ladle the sauce into jars.

HARVEST

Poetic phrases lose themselves in acres of hay,
evaporate in ripples of heat.
Neat windrows lie like finished sentences.

Days melt into weeks.
Forage neatly stacked,
I prepare for winter.

One frosty morning,
I open sweet-scented forage,
catch my breath, a verse remembered.

Captured.
I savor words with hot chocolate,
decorate paper with memory.

BRANCH OF THE FAMILY TREE

Grandma's receipts, decades old,
tuck among dance cards.
Embroidered pillowslips rest
under flour-sack aprons, wool socks,
bone hairpins. A simple wedding band
hides among her dainty hankies.

In her sewing box,
a brown button from her winter coat
lays among needles and thimbles—
nestled at the bottom a photograph.

Who is the man with owning arms
'round Grandma's waist?
Dark curly hair droops on his forehead.
She's smiling, hands rest upon his.

In her photo albums, she never smiles
beside Grandpa.

We almost miss the yellowed envelope
cushioned in Grandma's Bible.
Within, an obituary,
of an unknown man from Ireland.

THISTLES

Thistle gives me grief,
heartburn,
anxiety attacks.
I can't control Houndstongue,
Canada, Scotch, Musk.
They're Satan's weeds!

Some stick to everything,
poking holes in my clothes
and tender fingers, attach
to dogs, deer, livestock;
insidious seed borne on wind.

Thistle escapes into draws,
creekbeds, and meadows.
They thrive like managed crops.
I'm robbed of sleep thinking
of ways to root them out.

I buy insects to defend
garden, hayfields, and pastures.
I spray, cut, and cuss them.
Thistle lives and multiplies,
spreads worse than gossip in small towns.

SADDLEMAKER

In Memory of Jerry Croft

His roughened hands embrace the blade,
carve leather with the sure strokes of a man
who knows his trade. Laced fenders, tooled skirts,
a calf or cougar, to "purty it up."

Chew can tucks in his vest pocket.
Soiled Stetson snugs rust-red hair.
Gladrag faded, Wranglers stuffed in boot tops,
shirttail never quite tucked in.

He's known horse miles; reins easy in his hand, cow smart.
Eyes as blue as the rivers he's crossed.
His colorful stories paint our world
'til gravity and years take their toll.

I like to think of Jerry, a chew in his lip,
leaning on God's fence rail,
yarning with old cowboys and saddlemakers—
eyes alight and laugh lines creasing his cheeks.

THE SILVER BELLY

The silver belly hat lies in its box—
new, unsoiled, ready.

Robert's working felt is oiled with sweat,
stories concealed in creases and hollows.
A bur oak snagged that hole near the crown,
as he followed a bull through
the brush. He cursed the cigarette
that burned the brim and the wind
that sent it sailing into the reservoir.
The old hat soaked up rain, sunshine,
and snow, character set in folds of dust.

You can't tell its color but you know
the man who wears it has had a hard ride.

ACCIDENTS HAPPEN

Rime meets boot as I step into the stirrup,
clouds of breath meet a sullen sky.
Talons of winter clutch the land.
In the pasture, a young cow lays on her side,
labors with birth. Sixty yards away,
a comfortable shed bedded in straw.

I ride toward the heifer.

She rises, her calf in abnormal birth position.
I angle her toward the shed.
Halfway, she abruptly changes direction.
My mare wheels to follow and falls—
we slam onto the frozen ground,
both wheezing for air.

I'm pinned. Seconds pass
until my horse struggles to her feet,
quivering as I reach for the stirrup.
Leg pain explodes.
Many minutes later, numbed with cold
we begin travel to the ranch house.

Boot cut, limb packed with ice, my husband
leaves to assist the cow with delivery.
Two hours later, he reports mother and calf
are doing fine and adds, with a twinkle in his eye,
he did my job quite well. I grin too and reply,
he'll have to cook and clean . . . .

I'm sure I'll need weeks of recuperation.

ENCHANTMENT

Frost drapes trees in sequined dresses
ready for dawn's dance of lights.
Lodgepole, cedar, and oak listen
to the music of the wind.

Snowflakes begin the ballet,
pirouette into a waltz, sashay to a salsa.
Sunlight rims the hills, a strobe-light of color,
change of costume sweeps the landscape.

HOT DOGS BY CANDLELIGHT

Outside, evening drapes a heavy winter cloak.
Electrical lines frost, then sag. Drifts of snow
hide all landmarks. A hush settles.

I light candles. The wood in the fireplace
burns steadily. We skewer hot dogs, hold
them fast to flame, watch juices burst forth.

We speak softly of
   children,
   weather,
   ranching,
   marriage.

We celebrate moments for two,
hearts laced.

SALVAGE

The granary leans; plank walls weathered
a beautiful bronze streaked with black.
Foundation sandstones, carefully wedged,
crumble, as have lifetimes working the soil.

Three bins within held oats, wheat, barley,
before wind, snow, ice, and years,
spread the boards just enough to render
it useless for grain.

Mice and rats now hold dominion
over an old stove, cream cans, bedsprings,
and assorted bolts and nails. Floor boards
snap and break with each season.

In autumn breeze, we clear the refuse,
remove each plank with care,
panel the office walls with history,
the best of Christmas gifts.

KINFOLK

His grandchildren came today,
searched the courthouse records
for his claim, asked around town
for folks who might have known him.

Such a shame I missed their asking.
Could have shown them where his cabin stood,
guided them to the well he dug by hand,
led them to where he rests.

Might have shared a cup of coffee,
spoken of the old days ... their grandpa's
way with a horse. Oh, he could
ride them and sketch them.

Silence often his companion,
his actions spoke clearly to those
who shared his life.
When my saddle horse died,
he drew a charcoal in remembrance.

Now his family's left town.
No name or address,
no clue where they came from.
I wonder why, in all the years I knew him,
he never spoke of having kin?

Some silences last forever.

HEARTWOOD

The ground shudders,
limbs snap, as the ponderosa
meets the earth.
Silence surrounds. I kneel,
count her rings inside riddled bark—
one hundred twenty-two.

When a tree sprout,
long before bark beetle found this home,
Great-Granddad cleared ranch fields
of petrified wood, igneous rock,
sandstone inlaid with fossils.

When a sapling,
Wyoming became a state.
Grandma was born the year
this tree was twenty summers strong.
In evergreen maturity, buried in snow
halfway up her trunk,
she withstood the winter of '49.

As I cradled my great-grandson,
the ponderosa's needles were dying.
She stood one last winter,
dignity ravaged,
little bark to protect her core.

I grieve the conifer's loss and wonder;
who will note our passing,
who will count our years?

DROUGHT

PRAIRIE RECLAMATION

Swings hang empty
among bronzed stems of grass.
A slide sinks in plains dirt.
A derelict lilac stands guard
at the outhouse door,
which creaks in a breeze
the windbreak cannot catch.
Shingles lie scattered.
Windows and roof gape.

Inside the school, desks lie abandoned.
Floorboards, burdened in dust, lean south
from the shift of rock foundation.
A world map is severed at the equator.
South America, Africa, and Australia
droop in tatters, books strewn beside them.
A cast-off alphabet hangs
above the neglected blackboard.
Long-ago recitations linger in prairie wind.

FOR SALE

Our neighbor shuffles along the sidewalk,
ninety-four years behind him.
One foot cocks to the right,
a lesson from a salty eight-year-old gelding
with a penchant to buck.
Legs bowed from saddle miles,
he peers beneath his sweat-stained hat.
Town-ridden, not allowed to drive,
to have his dog, to eat what he wants—
doctors dictate his life.

He misses his birthplace,
the house grandad built,
home to youth, marriage, and children.
He talks to his long-dead mother at night,
while the town slumbers.
Cattle drives, grain threshing, stacking hay
canter through his dreams as departed neighbors
meet at branding fires. He's young, virile,
filled with plans for the future.

The drive to the ranch stirs his blood,
fills his lungs with a breath of pine.
At the corrals he complains of grit in his eyes,
his handkerchief wipes away decades of memories.
The house lists west, yawning in sunshine
as he peeks through a small bedroom window
where his children were conceived; his children,
who now print sale bills cataloging his life's work.

EMPTY HARNESS

Chalk Eye, our aged gelding,
droops his massive head lower
to nuzzle my cheek.
Bones, Chalk Eye's brother,
stands near.

The vet casts the words
into the chill air—bone disease.
Against all odds,
both of them.
Tears scald my cheeks.

Weeks later, a backhoe
gashes prairie sod. The motor stills.
I lead the sorrels
to where they will rest—
companions always.

I flinch as each shell
clicks into the chamber,
shudder at the rifle's reports.
Removing their halters,
I begin the long walk home.

DISCARDED

Dust devils ride empty reservoirs,
lope across barren hayfields, trot into corrals,
canter away into pines rimming the hillside.

Torrid temperatures desiccate grasses.
No birds burst forth with song.
No livestock or wildlife graze.

Abandoned buildings do not welcome.
Their ranch sign swings by one hinge,
a gust away from letting go.

FRIED BREAD

In Memory of Mother-in-law Frances

Hand-me-down dresses hung on her Depression-poor frame.
Weekends she wore coveralls, bottoms rolled up
obliging short legs. Her daddy walked away one day
when she was eight, so Mama married his brother. Months later
Baby Sister came into her care.

Older siblings argued over who milked cows,
churned butter, fed chickens, hoed the garden.
Then Mama died. Age twelve, she assumed command
of the wood stove, cooking stew, pork hocks and beans
but fried bread became the family favorite.

Eighteen, tall and blonde, she married her sweetheart—buried him
eight years and two children later. She cooked for a wealthy family,
tended bar, met a man, and left her kids with her old-maid aunt.
Bright lights, hard men, and harder whiskey took their toll.
At her funeral, all agreed, nothing compared to her fried bread.

TRANSFER

A slender trifold paper confirms ownership
of Block 8, Lot 2 in Mount Moriah Cemetery.
The town clerk and mayor penned their names
to that long-ago purchase.

The weight of paper has changed,
becomes a gift never meant to be given,
to our daughter, who has no plot
in which to bury her only child.

HOLLOW

In Memory of Taylor Robert Nixon; *too young to say goodbye.*

Blackbirds gather,
their calls disrupt the quiet of an overcast day.
Scarlet, umber, and gilded leaves nestle in ravines,
a womb for next year's Spring. A grasshopper, sole survivor,
moves sluggishly to the next blade of wind-burnt grass.

Bronzed grasses ride the edge of a well-worn trail,
leading to her family's favorite place.
Under her ribs, quivering heart muscle
craves suspension, release, peace.

Is it possible to wear down pain, walk it into the ground?
How long until sunlight melts the icy hollow in her heart?

EUTHANASIA

I pull Buddy's quivering body closer
as the vet draws the solution into the syringe.
The months of puppy tracks, eaten toys,
and cuddles cascade through memory—
as do the three people whose skin he's pierced.
There cannot be a next time.

My former boss holds the syringe,
asks if I am sure. Nodding, my fingers
burrow into my dog's sleek black hair.
I avoid Bud's trusting brown eyes,
gulp away tears when he whimpers with fear.
Never has doing the right thing,

felt so gut-wrenchingly wrong.

THE MILLIONAIRE

Barn wood pulls away.
Loosened square-head nails reveal gaps
where skunks and coons make entry.
His family's brand, white against barn red,
splinters in the sun and corral posts lean far to the south.

He sits in a long-used recliner,
once-bright blue eyes sunken.
Flaccid flesh of upper arms belie muscular youth,
A pot belly hides a worn leather belt.
Swollen feet and ankles no longer fit weathered boots.

His hands fought at Iwo Jima,
hammered boards, shod horses,
knotted rope, caressed a woman.
Now they lie still in his lap as his mind works his misery.

He remembers the Depression,
working the land Grandpa claimed,
burying Ma beside Pa when he was twelve,
holding on through the dust, drought, and pain.

Married a good-working woman
who bore him two sons; both gone
to work the oilfield for a paycheck,
good times, and freedom.

He wonders where his wife went,
after forty-one years of skimping.
He hollered, "She'll be back!"
But that was ten years ago. Now, the money he hoarded
pays for his care from a woman he doesn't even know.

BAPTISM

In Memory of My Grandmother

She stands by the open Kansas grave,
baby sister in her twelve-year-old arms.
No tears yet for her mother,
in the pine box below.
No time for sorrow.

Milk cows, skim the cream,
churn butter, feed the baby, the chickens,
clean the soddy,
launder by washboard, haul wood . . . .
Dad's gone for weeks looking for work.
Neighbors haul her cream and eggs to town,
ask how she and Daddy are doing.
She says, "Just fine,"
though she's terrified of every night alone.

Salvation's the Bible,
not because she believes in God anymore,
but stories carry her day.
She's Daniel, in the den fighting
the rooster with spurs as long as her hand.
She's Noah, when rain falls for four days,
prairie sea grass floats 'til sun devours
the moisture. She's Jesus, in the wilderness,
but she doesn't call God to save her.

Her grandmother does—
takes her home to food, warmth, sanctuary.
In winter firelight Grandmother reads
about deliverance.

CORONER'S REPORT

In the dim hallway of the nursing home,
he glances into the dining room where
two residents doze; another, in a neck brace,
leans to the side of her chair.

A man in pajamas
sits in a wheelchair, his black Stetson
tipped forward, concealing his eyes.
A silver-haired woman hums to herself.

Time has paused here. Only the calendar records
a new year. Faded curtains match the faded faces
of those who exist hour to hour, day to day.
Weariness has found a haven, refuses to leave.

He walks on toward the room
where his neighbors now reside,
pauses. Today, their son passed away—
gun in hand, left no doubt the cause of death.

He pushes the door inward,
into soft lamplight,
profoundly sad as their eyes light up,
thinking he has come for a friendly visit.

Second Wind

WIDOW'S WAIT

In Memory of Elsie

Unremembered daughters come,
comb her hair, kiss her cheek,
hold her hand. She doesn't mind,
her thoughts are years away.

Her body bent with age and disease,
she watches the window for a glimpse
of him, smooths the wrinkles
in her tired blue dress, pats her hair.

Almost hidden between the folds
of loose skin, a band of silver and gold,
filigree worn smooth as is the word
inscribed: *Forever.*
She waits.

Pills taken, bed rails raised,
she whispers to him of unknown rooms,
nameless people, strange food—
hopes he'll come for her soon.

BITTERSWEET

At dawn she slips through bur oak to the chokecherry bush.
Yesterday's heat dwells in draws, lies in mown hayfields.
From a precarious perch she leans toward the hanging fruit.
Nimble fingers, purpled by juice, strip small berries
into a bucket dangling from her arm. Bees buzz,
sip nectar from late summer flowers.

She casts a glance toward the grassy bottom of the ravine,
remembers a heat-filled afternoon, buckets of berries cast aside,
youth and desire reaping another harvest.

Tears and sweat mingle as she returns to her pickup,
gaze resting on the ranch house in the distance. By now
his nurse has cleaned and fed him, watching for recognition
that never comes. She hopes he's calm today, wonders
if his vacant mind remembers the taste of chokecherries.

ATLAS
2013 South Dakota Blizzard

Whiteout.
Winds gust seventy miles per hour.
Thirty-four inches of snow blanket autumn fields,
suffocate livestock.

The rancher rides, searches for stock he might save.
His horse lurches through heavy drifts,
draws deep draughts of air with every step.
Chill rides their bones.

Snowmelt.
One hundred eight cows and calves are heaped in draws,
fifty-six frozen near a granary,
ninety-one huddled by windbreaks . . . all dead.

Two cows bawl into a gray dawn.
Hope recedes; bitterness takes its place.
Years of labor lie in prairie grass.
Rotting carcasses won't meet the loan.

END OF THE SEASON

I run my fingers through tangled mane.
This mare has given many foals
with gentle spirit, solid quarters,
wide chest and sound legs.

She's pastured with our old stallion
for fifteen years. He died last month.
Her grieving matches mine.
She carries his offspring one last time.

I remove the burs from her tail,
notice cataracts and the sway of her back.
Never thought she'd foal this late in life—
a last gift.

Someday I'll bury her beside her mate.
For now, I'll give her an extra ration of grain,
an extra measure of love,
and pray for a sorrel filly like her mama.

CONGESTIVE HEART

Fall has thrown away summer's dance card,
beckons a new partner with her show of colors.
Buttery leaves gambol across meadows,
slip into ravines, nestle for a lingering nap.

Multi-shades of grey steal across blue heavens.
Ponderosas shiver in a sharpening breeze.
Deer and antelope gather, elk bugle,
squirrels scurry to their treasure of stores.

Turkeys strut, plumage spread in lingering light.
Mice burrow and crickets sing their chorus.
Coyotes hunt a den, their plaintive cries
linger on the landscape.

For you and I dear love,
each hour, each day and night,
brings your ragged breath
near a final winter hibernation.

YEARS SLIPPED AWAY

The bedroll's warm and my breath plumes in the air.
Far above, a comet jets its way across the stars.
Shivering, I pull jeans over long-johns. Booted, I stumble
to the creek, fill the coffee pot while my husband kindles a fire.
He saddles the bay and buckskin while dawn
grays the sky over the Bighorn Mountains.

Bacon and eggs sizzle. Coffee warms our throats, cups heat
our hands. We make sandwiches, stuff them into saddlebags.
The bay's back is humped and he crow-hops as soon as I mount.
We separate, ride different canyons. An elk bugle
raises the hair on the back of my neck. Three cows graze on my left.
I move them toward the corrals a mile away. Quaking aspen gold
peek among lodge pole pine. I sweep pine needles from my saddle.

A crack of thunder startles me awake, shatters the dream,
the memory of years slipped away.

WIDOWMAKER

After fifty-four years, autumn fits your leaving.
Lifeless leaves curl and wither.

In a resolute wind, I scatter your ashes
among grasses you nurtured all your life.

Our bed drapes in winter-cold sheets.
Memories gather in a house too small for grief.

Dear as remember'd kisses after death, . . .
Deep as first love, and wild with all regret;
O Death in Life, the days that are no more.
Alfred, Lord Tennyson

DEPARTURE

I calendar the days of desolation.
Today, I threw away his toothbrush,
one hundred three days
      after he left ...
not to the doctor, not to the hospital,
not to the lake with his fishing pole.
I grab his robe and thrust my face
into the folds of captured scent
      but it is fading.

LILACS

Lilacs and pines, solidly rooted,
belong where the journey ends.
Plastic flowers seem out of place
among prairie grasses bent with breeze
whose music sings to lost souls
wandering among the headstones.

Some memorials stand in military precision.
A few are fenced, as they were in life.
Still others lean, as if to blow away,
leave no trace.

Yours, my love, is solid granite,
above a blanket of Kentucky Blue
carefully trimmed each month.
I kneel beneath the lilacs
and tell you of my life.

DREAM WATCH

I softly call your name as I slip into the stand of wheat,
fifty-five acres of gold.
Careful not to shell the seed, my aged hands
push ripened stems aside.

You must be here for you love the fullness of a crop.
Yards further, I call again.
The hawk above must wonder
at the trails through the field.

Did you leave with the winnowing scythe,
the burning heat of August?
For some good reason, I cannot find you here,
amid the nightly dreams and tear-damp pillow.

FRESH GRASS

YESTERDAY'S SOLDIERS

They gather each morning at the local coffee shop,
sit in retro chairs at scarred wooden tables,
share news of the latest battles
across the globe—grandchildren in harm's way
the first topic of lengthy conversation. Next,
they dissect politics with the skill of surgeons.

Silver-grey hair curls over the large ears
of a sunburned man with heavy jowls
and shrapnel-scarred arms. He punctuates election
news with thuds of his cup on the table.
Others nod conservative heads in agreement,
disparage Washington bureaucrats.

A cadence of voices continues. Fragrant coffee
fills the air. One man in bib overalls adjusts
a ball cap above his weathered brow,
limbers a speech about those who dodged the draft.
The town's barber cleans his glasses,
speaks of fishing when his boy returns from Iraq.

A former coach declares this season
will be the best they've seen in years. Six seniors
and that Johnson kid, the best arm in the whole state.
The banker, a flag on his lapel, shares his senior year
football disaster. Good-natured insults
and laughter entwine. Feet shuffle, throats clear.

Outside, on the cracked sidewalk, they hitch their pants,
prolong goodbyes, and drift away to daily routines.
They'll be here tomorrow, exchange the same stories
of long-ago wars, the cost of Medicare, price of gas,
the way the world's going to hell in a handbasket,
except for grandkids and good fishing holes.

RED-HEADED TROUBLE

His stubborn beak hammers
the steel-sided house. He drums for a mate—
I hope he gets a headache.

The abandoned bunkhouse, barn,
wooden posts; former targets,
all bullet-riddled, Al Capone style.

Ponderosa pines cover the hillsides;
this bird prefers buildings and the garden
laden with raspberries, earthworms, and seeds.

Now the apple trees—
a mistake of profound proportions.
Two holes drilled and a third begun

before he's chased to a fencepost.
Retribution. Capone-style.
There will be no funeral.

DUSK

I rest in a field of grass, observe a scurrying mouse,
listen to the whoosh of the owl seeking supper.
Sun-warmed earth soothes my aging limbs.
Crickets chirp for mates in the waning light of dusk.
Frogs croon for partners, summer romance blossoms.

I want to hold this moment close,
sip the nectar of peace and tranquility
as ponderosas darken on the ridge above.
Too soon, the moonrise will cast its light,
sharpen the landscape, bear the ghost of loneliness.

BIGHORN MOUNTAINS

Sunflowers spill down a southern slope
into the grassy meadow laden with lupine.
A porcupine lumbers toward a pine tree,
his cambium lunch. Gliding the thermals,
the red-tailed hawk pursues his meal.

Months pass.

Squirrels sense change in the air,
scurry to pack their stores in an old stump,
their chatter joined with chipmunks and jays.
Blackbirds group on fences and power lines.
Seed and grain swell their middles.

A black bear, cubs in her belly,
scavenges season's berries.
As gold and scarlet leaves curl and fall,
a whitetail gathers his harem of does.

When snow-layered silence blankets the night,
Listen to an ancient pine
falling,
falling

Away

The chair waits for her feather-light frame
to settle into the green cushion.
A wide window beckons, her favorite place
to watch spring burst into summer,
autumn fall to winter's breath.

The rocker doesn't move,
no slippered toes tuck beneath the footstool.
A favored book unfinished,
her cup of tea not brewed.

She must have slipped through the glass
into the needled forest, seeking an old friend
she hasn't seen in years.

The Last Mile

Thirty-one miles of country road
Eleven ranches, eight widows—

Three never kept a checkbook.
Two never set foot in the barn.
One lost the land to repossession.

The last one,
my friend,
couldn't take it anymore.

WEAKNESS IN THE MIND

Soft brown curls escape, frame her wistful face.
He's having an affair she tells us, with Ms. So-and-So.
Surely she's wrong; he's not that kind of cowboy.
She's tired, just imagining things, we say,
knowing her family's weakness in the mind.

Seasons ensue. We bring casseroles to her husband
as he grieves. We'll all miss her. A month later,
he and Ms. So-and-So are seen holding hands
at a movie in a distant town—coincidence of course.
He's not that kind of cowboy.

A Mother's Will

Dripping branches brush the window.
Days of rain threaten to flood the nest
her body protects. A tiny orange feather
fluffs against the breeze,
instinct battles chill air.

Is she hungry?
Earthworms inch
across the driveway,
avoid rivlets of water cutting
tributaries in the gravel.

Nightfall finds me listening
as raindrops cease.
I slip into restless sleep.
Sunrise finds her feeding offspring,
the driveway empty of worms.

AWAKENING

Sweet sage perfumes the cemetery.
I wash your smooth ebony headstone,
then our grandson's. I notice
the bees droning around the lilacs,
and breeze unfurling small flags
at resting places across this hilltop.

Scarlets, pinks, golds
layer the horizon. How many sunsets
have I missed since you passed?
How long since I thrilled to the call
of the meadowlark or tasted tart raspberries?
How long since I've shed tears of life, not death?

At home, I step from the car,
breathe deeply of fresh-cut hay.
Senses heightened,
starlight soft against my skin,
I embrace a second wind.

RIDING THE EDGE OF GOODBYE

I take my time saddling the buckskin mare.
This will be our last ride—
we're being turned out to pasture by loving family.

She swells her belly as I tighten the cinch,
so the saddle will slip when I mount—
seven decades of riding say otherwise.

I scratch behind the velvet ears,
her stomach muscles relax,
I pull the cinch snug.

Smiling, I lead her from the barn,
bring her to a stand,
swing astride and ride

to a meadow that spills into the valley.
On the reservoir a mallard swims toward the reeds
where his mate paddles close to their brood.

A fawn hidden in tall grass startles us.
It bounds away and I rein the mare
toward the ponderosa-clad slope.

I breathe in alfalfa and sage, breathe out sadness—
our youth has slipped away, yet gratitude remains
for sunrise and sunset shared.

We turn toward home.
Seasons of memories will sustain me
while my partner grazes her years away.

TENDING WILD HORSES

Hoarfrost glitters,
night etched with silence.
Moonlight shapes hillsides,
carves icy landscapes.

Echoes of hooves
spill out of a canyon,
shatter the midnight,
scatter the moonbeams.

Bays, sorrels, pintos
plunge down the gullies,
fling snow to woodland
beside ghostly trails.

Yesterday's cowboys,
shimmering shadows,
follow through starlight
drift into night.

DELIVERING FLOWERS TO THE NURSING HOME

Smiles wreath faces, even those with dementia—
colorful petals awaken a lonely day.
Wrinkled hands caress the posies,
Furrowed brows smooth. Memories stir.

Cloudy eyes rise to the basket
filled with blue and lavender pansies,
a gift for Martha who no longer knows
her husband or sons.

Delia tells me to leave her room,
then sharply says, "Wait! Are those daisies
for me?" She raises her arms
to embrace the bouquet, then weeps.

Alice, in a wheelchair, holds her baby doll close,
beams as I pin a corsage of roses to her
faded pink dress. I leave a vase of Stargazer lilies
for the staff, from an unknown—

the gift as sweet as the scent
wafting across the room
where Myriam, a former nurse,
slumps in the blue chair unaware of the day.

SOLSTICE

I reach for December sunlight,
hold its warmth, store it
against January, February, March.

I gather my bones in a blanket,
warm them by the fire,
hide from winter's face

as Canada geese wing,
sleepy grass awakened by their call.
A trickle of melt turns into a river.

BENEDICTION

Forty-four years she's scrubbed.
Knees swell and throb.
Hours spent shining windows,
brightening toilets, sinks, and tubs.

Arthritic hands with bone-spurred knuckles
scribble checks on a dwindling account.
Winter storms rage as the coal bin empties.
Tea bags are used, used, and used again.

Yet every Sunday she walks seven blocks,
kneels in the pew she's known since a child.
Face lit with inner joy, she thanks God
for all the blessings she receives.

*Yet those who wait on the Lord will
gain new strength.*
Isaiah 40:31

TALISMAN

Meadowlark melody beckons a mate. For a month
you court and claim, defend your land from intruders.
Busy with feeding the young, your melody silent.

Fledglings find their wings, fly low,
glide, flap with short, stiff beats,
cavort across the meadow near their mother's nest.
Their beaks lance the soil, grasp the seed, or bore the berry.

Too soon, western winds bring snow and you'll gather,
wait for storms to pass. I'll wait as well, for your song
to pierce frost-edged air, a talisman of spring.

RETREAT

The ranch house is unusually quiet.
Curled on the couch, seated at desks,
nestled in chairs, all immersed,
nine women lean into their writing.

Precious minutes pass, time carved
away from husbands, children, business.
We women gift ourselves moments
stacked neatly like the paper covered in ink.

We greet sunset seated at Grandmother's
oak table, hands joined in blessing.
Soft voices and laughter gain momentum,
our stories passed like plates of dessert.

SEASONED

Like paint peels away from wood,
my exterior gives way to age.
Juices of youth dry in summer breeze.

Early on, passions crashed
against the shoreline,
ebbing and flowing.

Vitality boundless,
I embrace winds of change,
destined for perpetuity not antiquity.

Mid-life pulse,
a gentle slope of hunger,
settling.

Now, within,
the fountain trickles,
occasionally rushes forth in exuberance.

My age is an old coat
to be cast off in private moments,
abandoned to receive autumn.

COWBOY CAFE

Locals gather to chew much the same fat as yesterday,
hats tipped back on balding hairlines.
Coffee mugs steam as boot heels hook on chair rungs,
mud and manure flaking onto the well-worn oak.

Scarred tables and chairs bear the weight of stories,
gossip, and laughter. Walls are covered with memories.
Ancient rodeo photos and posters ride beside
a blackboard menu and fading signage.

Mom and Pop own this outfit; been here since '69.
They've seen many cowboys come and go.
Mom's limping some and Pop, well, he still treats
little ones to candy he keeps in a jar beside the till.

Strong coffee, biscuits and gravy, and faithful friends
go a long way to make a good day.
Some say the times are changing too fast.
This cafe stays the same. Folks like it that way.

WINTER GARDEN

My flower garden quilt,
a treasured gift,
covers the bed in red roses,
lavender lilacs, yellow daisies.
Florals rest on sky-blue cotton,
each hand-stitched with care.

I love the vintage,
drape the bouquets
around my chilly limbs
and ponder deft fingers,
shadowed by candlelight,
stitching through a winter solstice.

.

PRAYER STARS

I search for angels,
Northern Lights mark my path.
Cotton nightgown brushes against
dew-damp grass soft beneath my toes.
Prayer stars gather
in heavenly sanctuary.

Second Wind

WHO WOULD I BE IF
I DIDN'T HAVE A NAME?

Wisdom-edged woman in Levis,
lover of ponderosa, buffalo grass, and a cowboy,
collector of rock and bone.
Companion to grandchildren, sagebrush,
and a buckskin mare with velvet muzzle.
Driver of posts, stretcher of wire
on sweat-drenched, blue-sky days.
Seeker of calves in bur oak shade,
hidden springs of earth-cooled water.
Wide-hipped, opinionated,
callus-handed mother and friend.
Widow, poet-emerging,
looking for sweet grass and red-tailed hawks.

Acknowledgments
Previously Published Works

"Bequest," *Manifest West; Serenity and Severity*, University of
    Colorado Press, 2016
"Harvest," *Grassland Genealogy*, Finishing Line Press, 2009
"Kinfolk," *Wyoming Paintbrush*, WYOPoets Chapbook, 2007
"Heartwood," *Home*, Tall Grass Guild Anthology, 2016
"Transfer," *Show Us Your Papers*, Main Street Rag, 2020
"Bittersweet," Writer's Digest Poetry Contest, Fifth Place, 2013
"Departure," *Gyroscope Review* Online Journal, 2018
"Lilacs," Wyoming Writers, Inc. National Contest, First Place, 2006
"Dream Watch," *Gyroscope Review* Online Journal, 2019
"The Last Mile," *How It Looks from Here*, Nebraska Writers Guild
    Chapbook, 2019
"Riding the Edge of Goodbye," Women Writing the West, 2012
"Tending Wild Horses," *Loon Magic and Other Night Sounds*, Tall
    Grass Writers Guild Anthology, 2019
"Who Would I Be if I Didn't Have a Name," *Grassland Genealogy*,
    Finishing Line Press, 2009

Patricia Frolander is blessed to manage the family ranch in the Black Hills of Wyoming. She and her husband, Robert, who passed away three years ago, shared three children, seven grandchildren, and two great-grandchildren, all of whom live close to the ranch. At this stage of her life she prefers the padded office chair at her desk.

Patricia's first book, *Grassland Genealogy*, was published in 2009. Her second book, *Married Into It,* was published by High Plain Press in 2013 and garnered the National Cowboy and Western Heritage Museum's coveted Wrangler Award, the WILLA Award, and High Plains Book Awards among others. Frolander's self-published chapbook, *Between the West Pasture and Home*, was distributed in October 2019. Her poetry has been widely published in numerous anthologies and featured in journals, magazines, and newspapers over the past twenty-five years.

The text is eleven-point Berkeley Oldstyle Book
by the International Type Company.
Display type is Cyan by the Wilton Foundry and Missale AS Incana.
The book is printed on
fifty-five pound Nature's Natural,
a fifty percent post consumer recycled paper, processed acid free,
by Versa Press